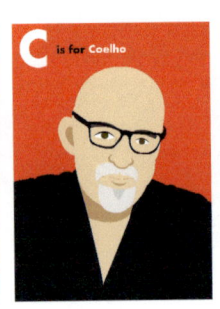

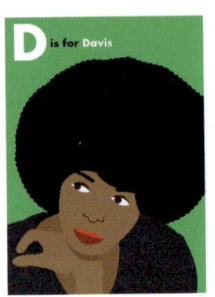

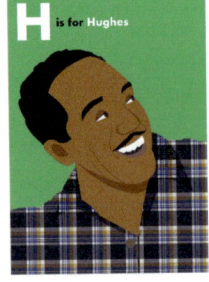

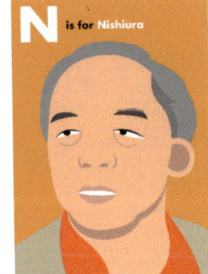

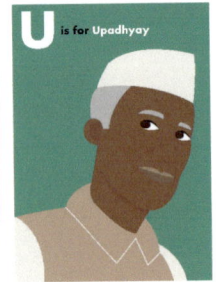

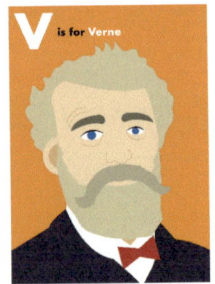

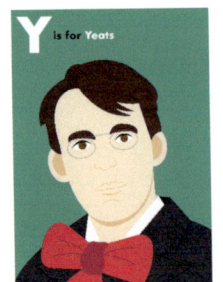

Z is for Zora
BY DR TAMARA PIZZOLI

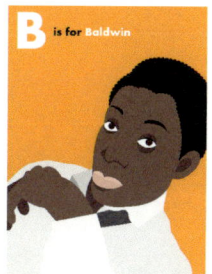

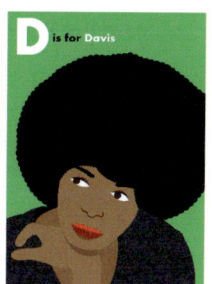

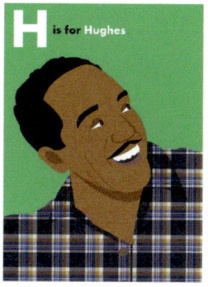

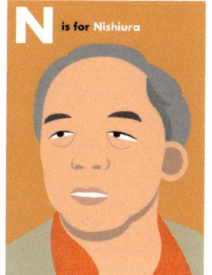

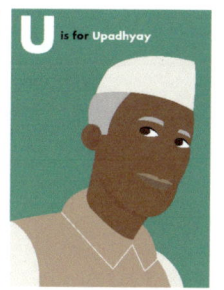

A is for Angelou	**B** is for Baldwin	**C** is for Coelho	**D** is for Davis	**E** is for Eugenides	**F** is for Frank
G is for Giovanni	**H** is for Hughes	**I** is for Ishiguro	**J** is for Jhumpa Lahiri	**K** is for Kaur	**L** is for Lewis
M is for Morrison	**N** is for Nishiura	**O** is for Ozeki	**P** is for Potel	**Q** is for Quinones	**R** is for Rowling
S is for Sanchez	**T** is for Twain	**U** is for Upadhyay	**V** is for Verne	**W** is for Walker	**X** is for Xinran
Y is for Yeats	**Z** is for Zora Neale Hurston				

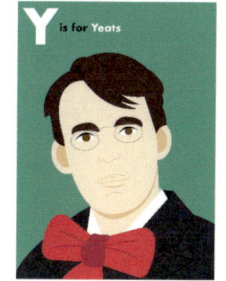

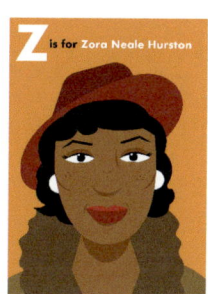

Z is for Zora
BY DR TAMARA PIZZOLI

For Noah, Milo, Zen and Lotus
and for my mom Katharyn and sister Nefeterius

www.theenglishschoolhouse.com

Text copyright © 2018 by Tamara Pizzoli
Pictures copyright © 2018 by Howell Edwards Creative
All rights reserved.

This book or any portion thereof may not be reproduced or used in any manner whatsoever without the express written permission of the author except for the use of brief quotations in a book review. This is a work of fiction. Names, characters, places, and incidents are a product of the author's imagination. Any resemblance to actual persons, events, or locales is entirely coincidental.

ISBN: 978-0-9976860-4-3

Z is for Zora

Dr. Tamara Pizzoli

Pictures by Howell Edwards Creative

THE ENGLISH SCHOOL HOUSE

A is for Angelou

B is for Baldwin

C is for Coelho

D is for Davis

E is for Eugenides

F is for Frank

G is for Giovanni

H is for Hughes

I is for Ishiguro

J is for Jhumpa Lahiri

K is for Kaur

L is for Lewis

M is for Morrison

N is for Nishiura

O is for Ozeki

P is for Patel

Q is for Quiñones

R is for Rowling

S is for Sanchez

T is for Twain

U is for Upadhyay

V is for Verne

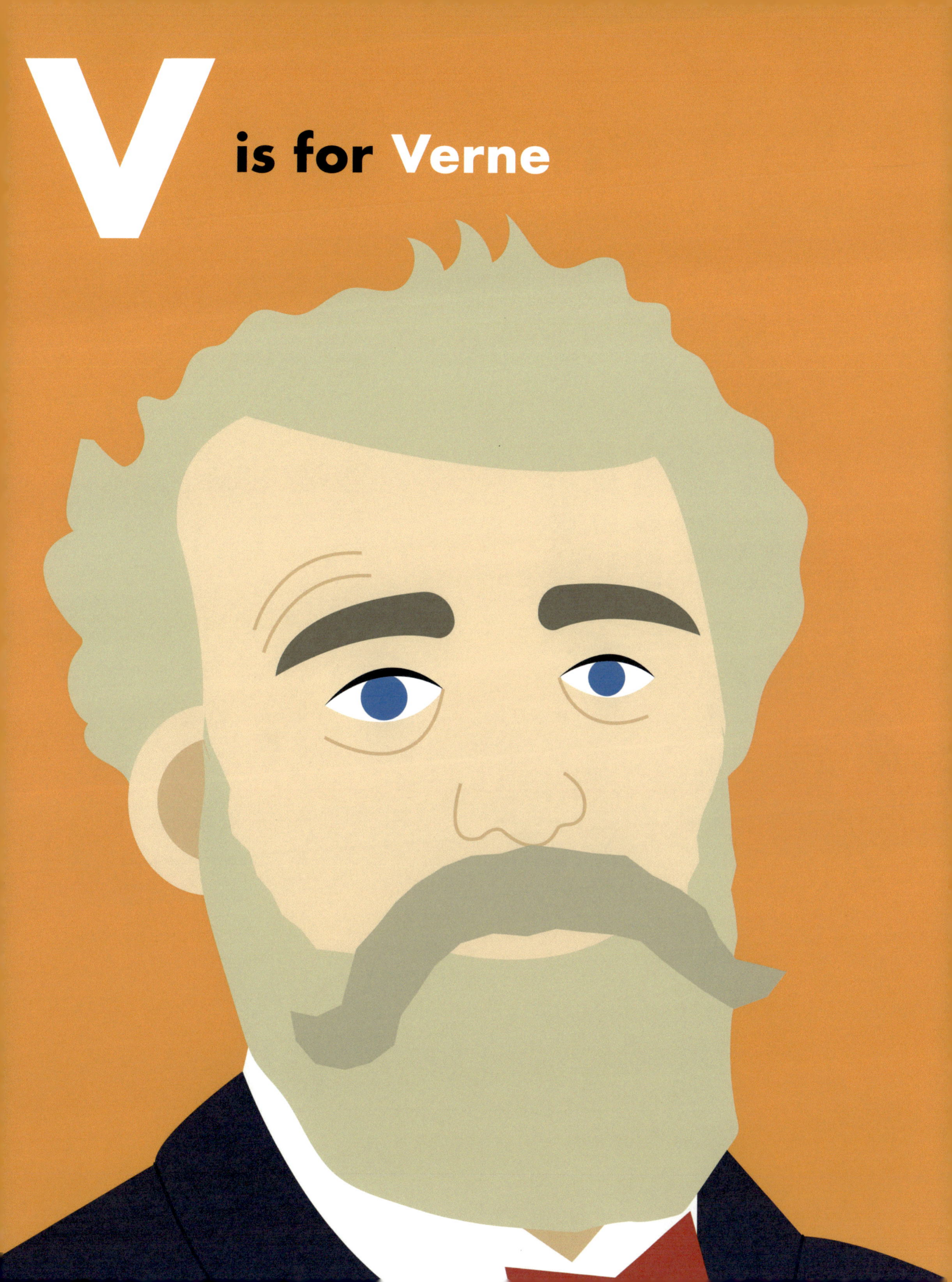

W is for Walker

X is for Xinran

Y is for Yeats

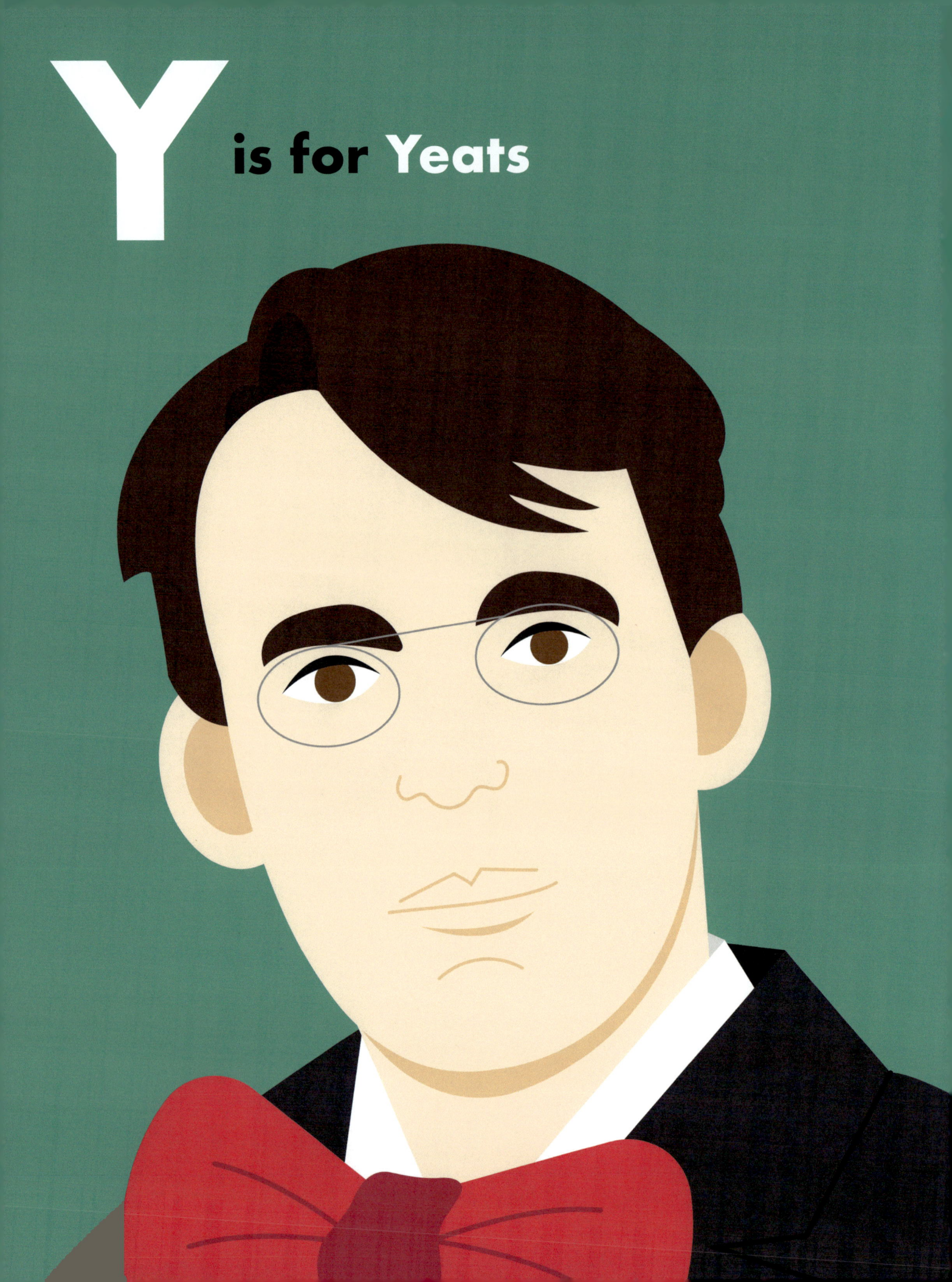

Z is for Zora Neale Hurston

Angelou, Maya Born in 1928, Maya Angelou is regarded as one of the most prolific poets of modern times. The efficacy of her words in written form earned Angelou more than fifty honorary degrees. Her first autobiography, *I Know Why the Caged Bird Sings*, is one of her most popular and widely read titles.

Baldwin, James Born in 1924, Baldwin discovered a love for literature arts and writing early in life. While still elementary school-aged, he penned both a play and the official song for his public school in Harlem. As an adult, Baldwin's writing explored themes such as religion, race and self identity. While in his early twenties, he expatriated to Paris, France.

Coelho, Paulo A native of Rio de Janeiro, Brazil, Coelho knew early on he wanted to become a writer. His childhood was marked with some serious adversity, including being committed to a mental institution, and during his early adult years Coelho lived through a range of experiences, from a stint in law school to traveling the world as a hippie. He published his first book in 1982 and just over a decade later found international success with his acclaimed novel *The Alchemist*.

Davis, Angela Originally from Birmingham, Alabama and born in 1944, Davis grew up attending segregated schools. She completed her formative education and attended Brandeis University in Massachusetts. Davis is considered not only one of the most important civil rights activists and revolutionaries in United States history, but an accomplished author, academic and scholar as well.

Eugenides, Jeffrey Eugenides was born in Detroit, Michigan in 1960. His decision to become a writer occurred while he was in middle school. He attended both Brown University and Stanford. The few novels that Eugenides has published have earned him international critical acclaim, numerous translations of his words into other languages and several awards for excellence in writing.

Frank, Annelies (Anne) Frank was born in 1929 in Germany but her family moved to Amsterdam, Netherlands when she was four years old. By 1940, Amsterdam had been occupied by German Nazis and the Jewish population was being persecuted. Frank and her family, like many Jews at the time, were forced into hiding. During that period, Frank wrote about her life experiences in a journal she'd received as a birthday gift. It was published after her untimely death under the title *The Diary of a Young Girl*.

Giovanni, Nikki Born in 1943 and named after her mother, Yolande Cornelia, Giovanni is considered today as one of the most recognized and noted African-American poets. Her writing covers social, political, and racial themes in a variety of mediums, including books for adults, children's literature and television programming. Giovanni's poems span over half a century and have been published in anthologies; she was even nominated for a Grammy Award in 2004 for Best Spoken Word Album.

Hughes, Langston Hughes was a native of Joplin, Missouri and was born in 1902. Raised primarily by his grandmother in Kansas, he found a love for books and expansive language early in life, and was elected class poet in grade school. As an adult, Hughes became a noted activist, poet and playwright.

Ishiguro, Kazuo Though he was born in Japan, Ishiguro's family relocated to England when he was a small child. He began his formal studies there, and focused on writing development during his university studies. Ishiguro has made a career as a successful novelist, even receiving the Swedish Academy's Nobel Prize in Literature.

Jhumpa Lahiri Lahiri's birth name is Nilanjana Sudeshna, but she goes by the nickname Jhumpa. Born in London in 1967, Jhumpa's family moved to the U.S. when she was two. In college she studied English, and her professional writing as a novelist has earned her numerous literary awards, including the Pulitzer Prize for Fiction.

Kaur, Rupi Kaur was born in India in 1992 and moved to Canada at the age of four. Kaur was drawn to poetry as a child, as well as drawing and painting. Her poetry is often accompanied by her own illustrations. Kaur's prose compiled in books have sold over two million copies and her first book, *Milk and Honey*, was a staple on the The New York Times Best Seller list.

Lewis, C.S. Lewis was born in 1898 in Ireland. As a child he was an avid reader, and as he grew into an older boy, he took an interest in mythology and Greek literature. As a professional writer, Lewis was heavily influenced by his Christian faith. One of his most popular contributions to the world of fiction is the widely adapted book *The Chronicles of Narnia*.

Morrison, Toni Morrison, who was born with the name Chloe Ardelia Wofford, entered the world in the year 1931. As a child, her parents retold African-American tales and songs to her, and Morrison developed a love for reading early. The nickname Toni came about during her adolescence. As an adult she focused on writing fiction stories. Her first book, *The Bluest Eye*, was published in 1970. She's penned more than a dozen novels, several children's books with her son, as well as a pair of plays. Her seminal work over the years has earned numerous prestigious awards, including the Nobel Prize for Literature.

Nishimura, Kyotaro Nishimura was born in Tokyo, Japan in 1930. He is most widely known in Japan as an award-winning writer of mysteries, both in novels and short stories. Some of his writing pieces have been translated and published in English.

Ozeki, Ruth Ozeki was born in 1956 and grew up in New Haven, Connecticut. She began her creative career in film and production in the mid-eighties, but by the late nineties had transitioned into writing novels. Her published work is award-winning and has been translated into over two dozen languages.

Patel, Shailja Patel was born in Kenya. She was raised in Nairobi and attended college in England before moving on to the United States. Patel's most widely read work is entitled *Migritude*, and with her words she explores concepts such as women's rights and issues, cultural issues and colonialism.

Quiñones, Ernesto Quinones was born in Cuba in 1970. His first book, *Bodega Dreams*, was published in 2000. *Chango's Fire*, his second novel, was published four years later. Quiñones has also made notable contributions to journalism, and he serves as a professor of English at Cornell University.

Rowling, J.K. Rowling's first name is Joanne, and she was born in England in 1965. She is a novelist, television producer and screenwriter who has written under the pen names J.K. Rowling as well as Robert Galbraith. Rowling's books have won several awards and are internationally loved and recognized, particularly the *Harry Potter* series, which propelled her from a period of living in near poverty to becoming the first author in the world to reach billionaire status.

Sanchez, Sonia Sanchez was born in Birmingham, Alabama in 1934. As a result of several unfortunate family events, she developed a strong stutter as a young child, but found refuge in books and literature arts. Her love for reading and writing led her to a professional career as both a poet and and a professor. She has written numerous award-winning books of poetry, and has been a professor at several universities. Recurring themes in Sanchez's work include the bond between mother and child and the African-American experience, and she is a staple in the discussion of civil rights and activism.

Twain, Mark Samuel Langhorne Clemens wrote and was published under the pen name Mark Twain. Born in 1835, Twain's published work eventually became literarily synonymous with examples of the height of excellence in American writing with novels such as *The Adventures of Tom Sawyer* and *Huckleberry Finn*.

Upadhyay, Harilal Upadhyay was born in India in 1916. He began writing early in life and had his first short story published in a magazine when he was only 15. After following an uncle who was a professional storyteller and collecting varied stories and songs from him, as well as learning the art of presentation, Upadyay began to write poems and short stories and novels in his adulthood. He penned over 100 books.

Verne, Jules Jules was born in 1828 in France. He was sent to boarding school at age six, and Verne was captivated by the stories that his teacher at the school would tell the class. By his teenage years he was quite serious about writing long prose, including essays and poetry. Though he held a law degree and at one point had the opportunity to take over his father's law practice, Verne earned prestige as a novelist and playwright with such classics as *Twenty Thousand Leagues Under the Sea* and *Around the World in Eighty Days*.

Walker, Alice Walker was born in Georgia in 1944 to a family of sharecroppers. After an accident involving a sibling left her blind in one eye, Walker immersed herself in the literary arts. She attended Spelman College and then Sarah Lawrence College. In addition to writing novels, essays and poetry, Walker was and continues to be outspoken on civil and women's rights. Her novel *The Color Purple* led to her being awarded the National Book Award as well as the Pulitzer Prize for Fiction. She is also credited with coining the term "womanist."

Xinran, Xue Xinran was born in China in 1958, and uses just her last name as a pen name. She was raised by her grandparents, and moved to London in the late nineties. She is credited with spearheading seminal work and writing dealing with women's issues, particularly in China. Her very first book, *The Good Women of China*, was featured on best-seller lists internationally.

Yeats, William Butler Yeats was born in Ireland in 1865. Later his entire family relocated to England, and Yeats struggled academically in certain areas in school but thrived in others. His first serious attempts at writing occurred in his late teenage years, and by his adulthood Yeats joined private clubs of poets who would meet to recite their prose. As one of the co-founders of the Abbey Theatre, Yeats is widely considered to be one of the most important contributors to literature in the twentieth century.

Zora Neale Hurston Born in 1891 in Alabama, Hurston's family relocated to Florida when she was just three. The deep south and the plight and truths of people of the African Diaspora were recurrent themes in her writing, which included short stories and essays, as well as plays. Her most widely read work was a novel published in 1937 entitled *Their Eyes Were Watching God*.

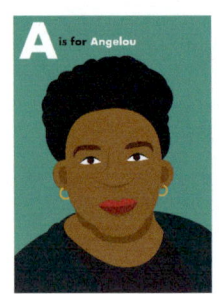

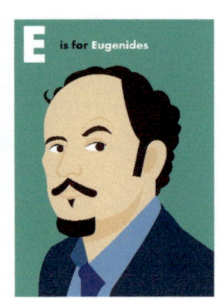

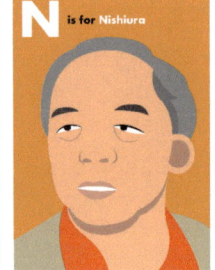

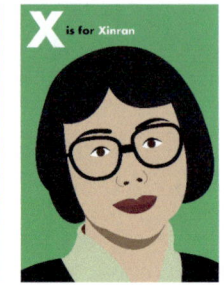

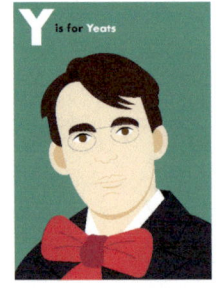

A is for Angelou	**B** is for Baldwin	**C** is for Coelho	**D** is for Davis	**E** is for Eugenides	**F** is for Frank
G is for Giovanni	**H** is for Hughes	**I** is for Ishiguro	**J** is for Jhumpa Lahiri	**K** is for Kaur	**L** is for Lewis
M is for Morrison	**N** is for Nishiura	**O** is for Ozeki	**P** is for Patel	**Q** is for Quinones	**R** is for Rowling
S is for Sanchez	**T** is for Twain	**U** is for Upadhyay	**V** is for Verne	**W** is for Walker	**X** is for Xinran
Y is for Yeats	**Z** is for Zora Neale Hurston				

Z is for Zora
BY DR TAMARA PIZZOLI

A is for Angelou	**B** is for Baldwin	**C** is for Coelho	**D** is for Davis	**E** is for Eugenides	**F** is for Frank
G is for Giovanni	**H** is for Hughes	**I** is for Ishiguro	**J** is for Jhumpa Lahiri	**K** is for Kaur	**L** is for Lewis
M is for Morrison	**N** is for Nishiura	**O** is for Ozeki	**P** is for Patel	**Q** is for Quinones	**R** is for Rowling
S is for Sanchez	**T** is for Twain	**U** is for Upadhyay	**V** is for Verne	**W** is for Walker	**X** is for Xinran
Y is for Yeats	**Z** is for Zora Neale Hurston				

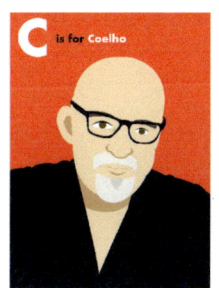

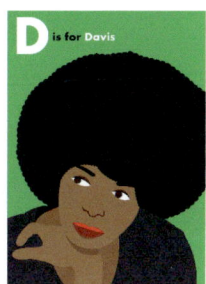

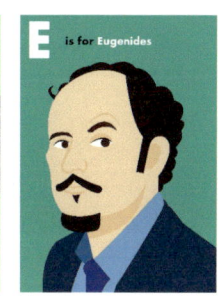

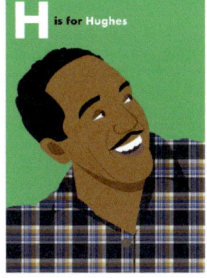

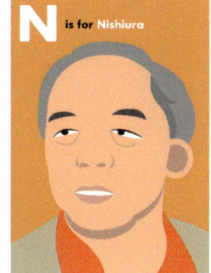

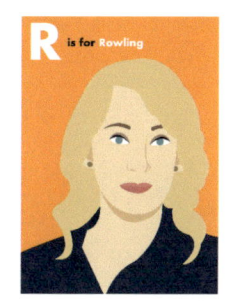

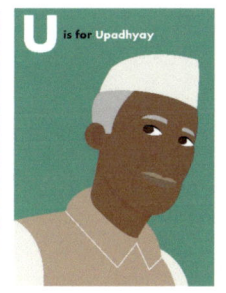

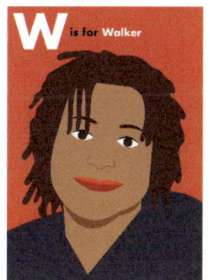

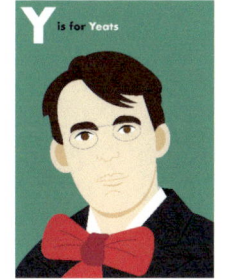

Z is for Zora
BY DR TAMARA PIZZOLI

Made in the USA
Columbia, SC
08 April 2025